The Unofficial Guide To A Messy INKTOBER
Year One

Created by **My Daily Hashtag Challenge**
Produced and Illustrated by **Ron Jones The Artist**
Published by **RenderBit Publishing**

Copyright © 2017 by Ronald B. Jones Jr
All rights reserved. Any distribution and reproduction of this book requires authorized permission from the copyright holder.

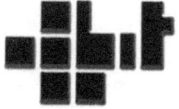

Intro

Welcome to your new favorite sketchbook

Hey there!

My name is Ron, short for Ron Jones The Artist. One day I realized life got away from me and I wasn't doing anything creative. Depression, relationships, day jobs, and the "impostor" syndrome can really mess with an artist. So one day online, I was reminded that Inktober was coming up. Feeling inspired, I promised myself I wouldn't procrastinate another year. There was a surge of dedication that took over me as I started looking at past entries. Then I found myself becoming obsessed with finding tips and inspiring illustrations. After a few days, I became a total internet guru, but I knew I needed to actually draw something to prove it to myself. Plus I still had a long time before Inktober even started. Knowing I was going to forget most everything I learned, I got the idea to write it in the sketchbook that I wanted to use. Then I had the better idea to use 31 different themes, and put it all in a handbook. Thus the collection of a messy Inktober was born!

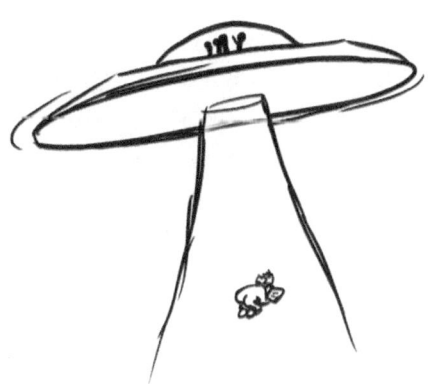

What is Inktober?!

What Inktober means to me is a 31 day challenge to test your monochromatic skills while experimenting with a specific tool set. Inktober's founder, Jake Parker, has plenty of videos and tips via his website, Inktober.com, and YouTube channel. Please go support and be sure to use the hashtag #Inktober to share with the community. Also my friends popularized the hashtags #CharacterADayChallenge and #MyDailyHashtagChallenge. We encourage a daily dose of drawing all year, so don't feel like you can only use this book in October.

Remember there're no rules, so no shame in disregarding the themes. Even if you want to draw on everything BUT the blank pages, we won't judge. Don't be afraid to make mistakes and get messy. If your fingers and toes stay clean all month, you're doing it wrong. There's an index in the back in case you and your page bleeds too much to see the next theme. To help... rip out the next page and put it under your daily work to make it bleed proof. Sparking your creativity under a constraint and accountablity are the reasons for doing this challenge. Post your work using your favorite hashtags, and email any feedback or suggestions to RenderbitPublishing@gmail.com. If you fall, get back up, keep going, and have FUN!!

Designated Bleed Prevention Page

Tools To Use

The tools don't make the artist, find what works and call it a style

Pens
Copic Multiliner
Pigma Micron Pen

Brush Pens
Pental Pocket Brush
Kuretake no. 13 Brush Pen

Brushes
Winsor & Newton Sable Brush

Fountain Pens
Speedball Dip Pen Set
Copic Black Drawing Pen

Ink
Higgins Black India Ink
Kuretake Sumi Ink

Other
Whiteout
Water
Paper Towels
Soup For Cleaning

Techniques

One man's line is another man's form

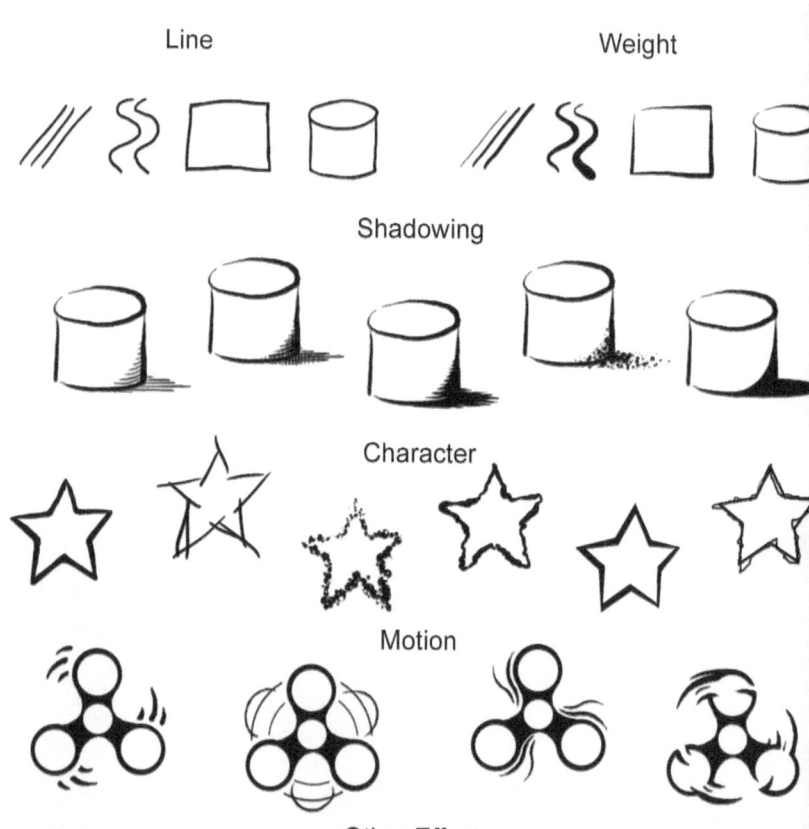

Other Effects
Ink Splatters
Water Marks
Smokey Burns
Stains and Smudges

#Inktober

Day 1
What is that in the mirror?

#CharacterADayChallenge

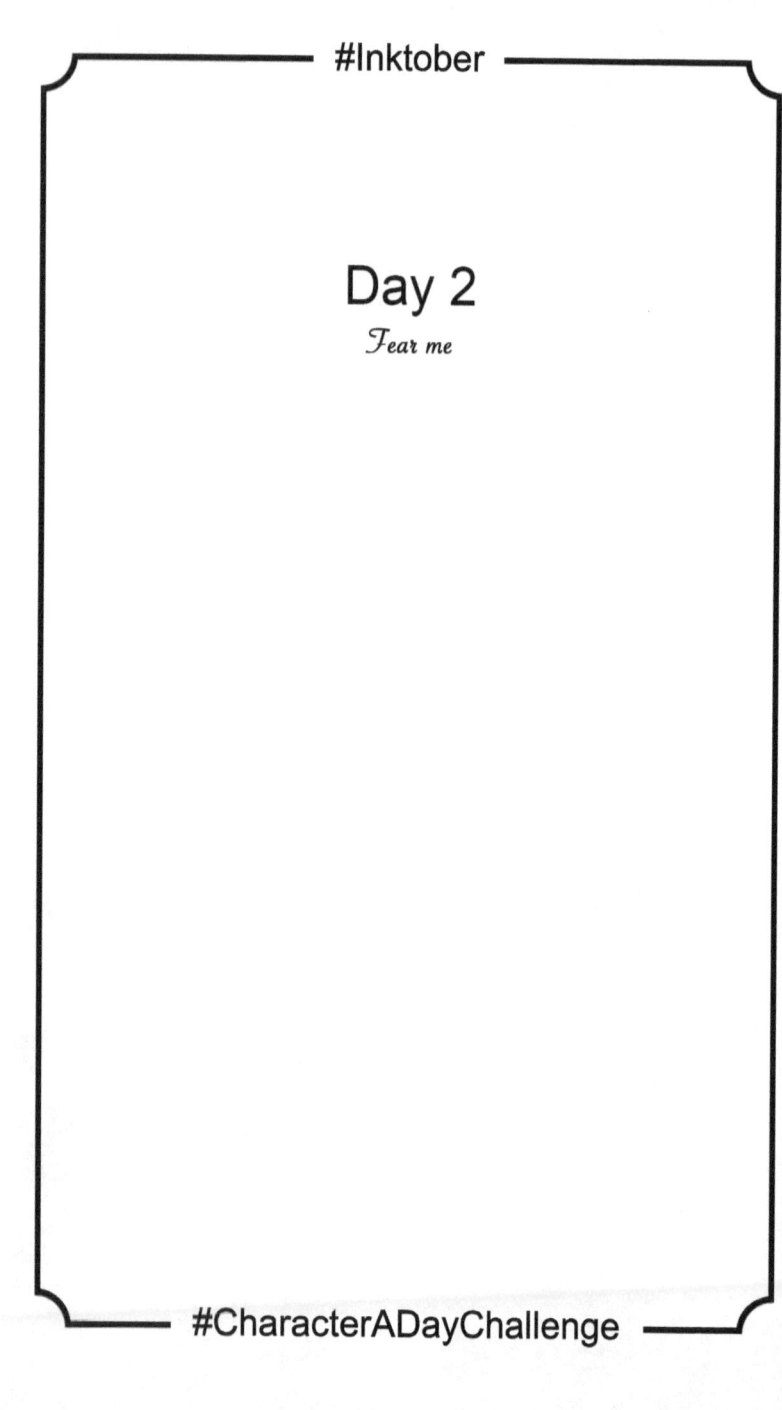

#Inktober

Day 3
Find the warrior maid of glasses

#CharacterADayChallenge

#Inktober

Day 4
It's always darkest before the dawn

#CharacterADayChallenge

#Inktober

Day 5
Food for thought

#CharacterADayChallenge

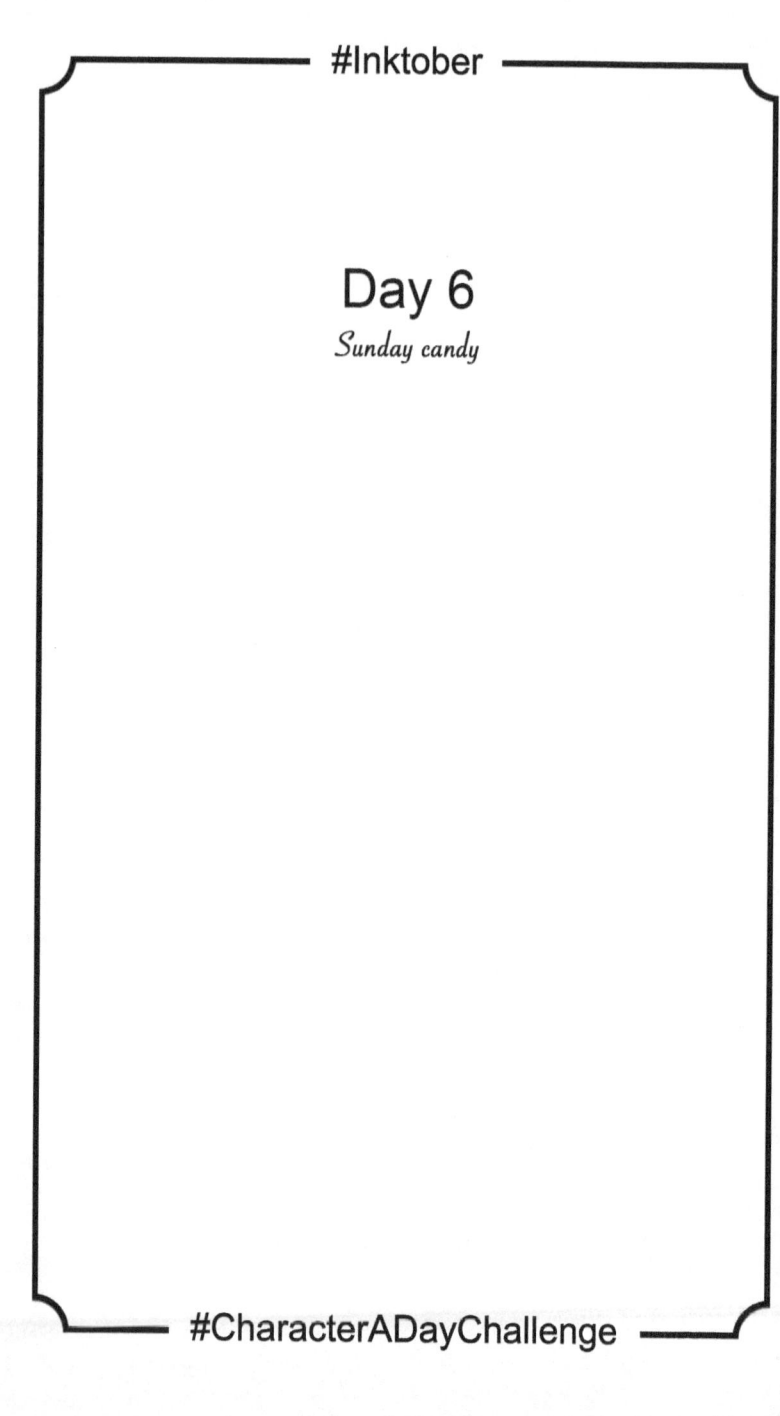

#Inktober

Day 7
Make your own sound bagel

#CharacterADayChallenge

Day 8
The deeper you are

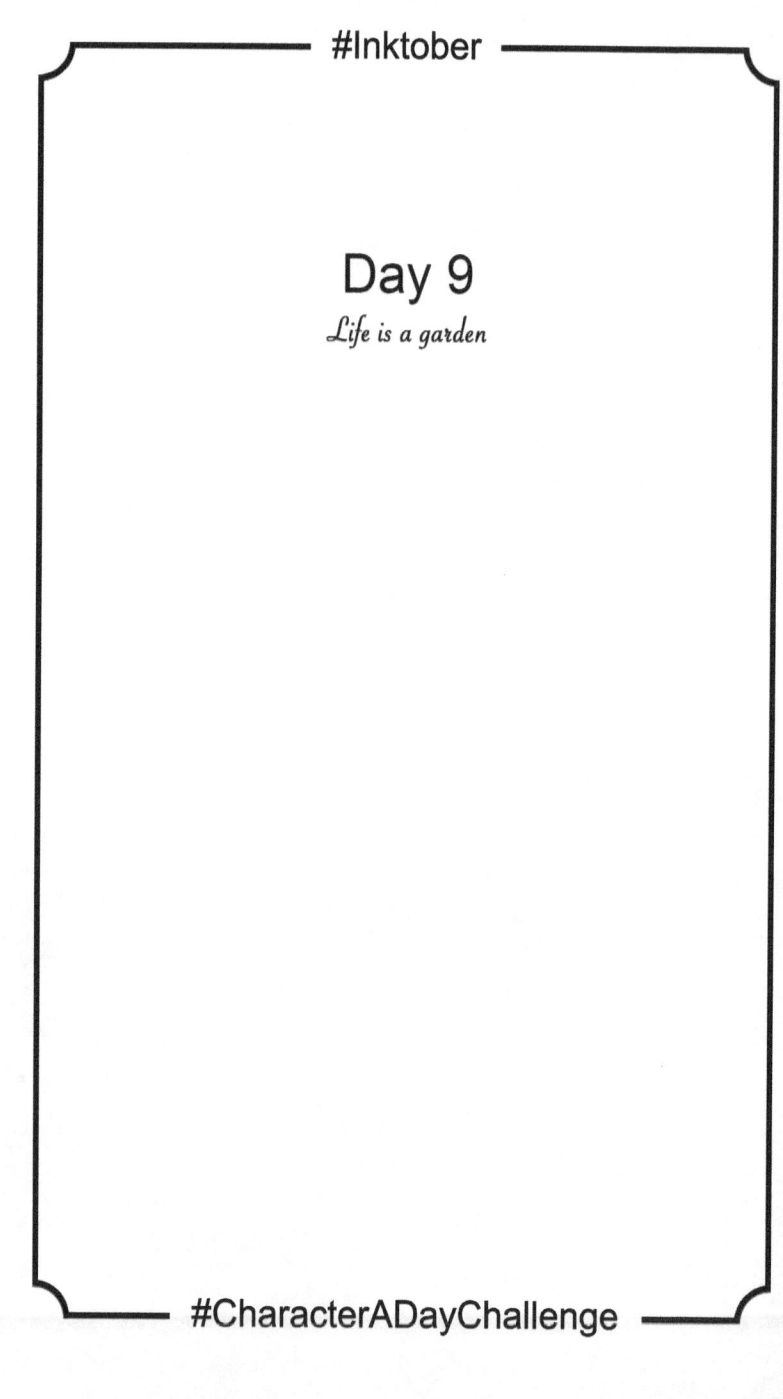

Day 9
Life is a garden

#Inktober

Day 10
Show me something natural

#CharacterADayChallenge

#Inktober

Day 11
These scars mean nothing

#CharacterADayChallenge

Day 12
I can see the finish line

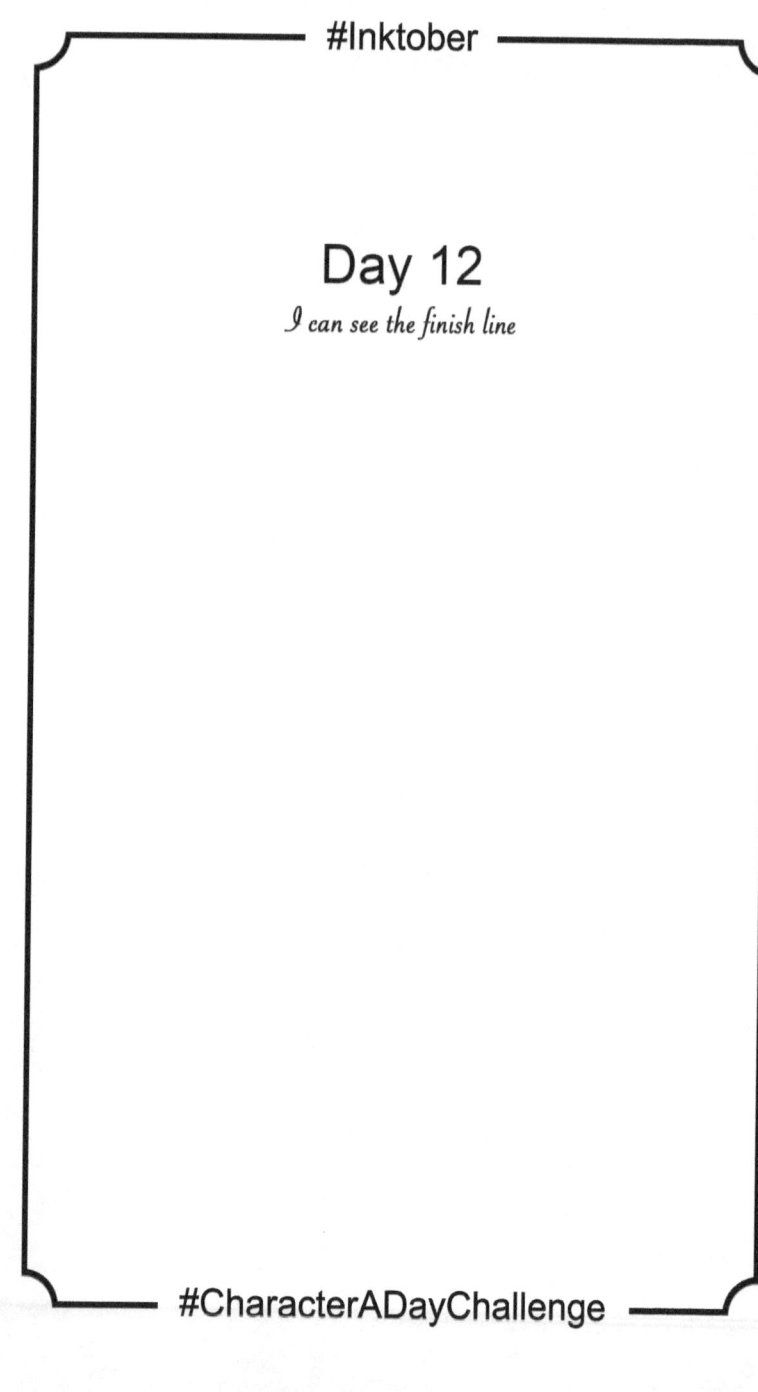

#Inktober

#CharacterADayChallenge

#Inktober

Day 13
Pick your superpower

#CharacterADayChallenge

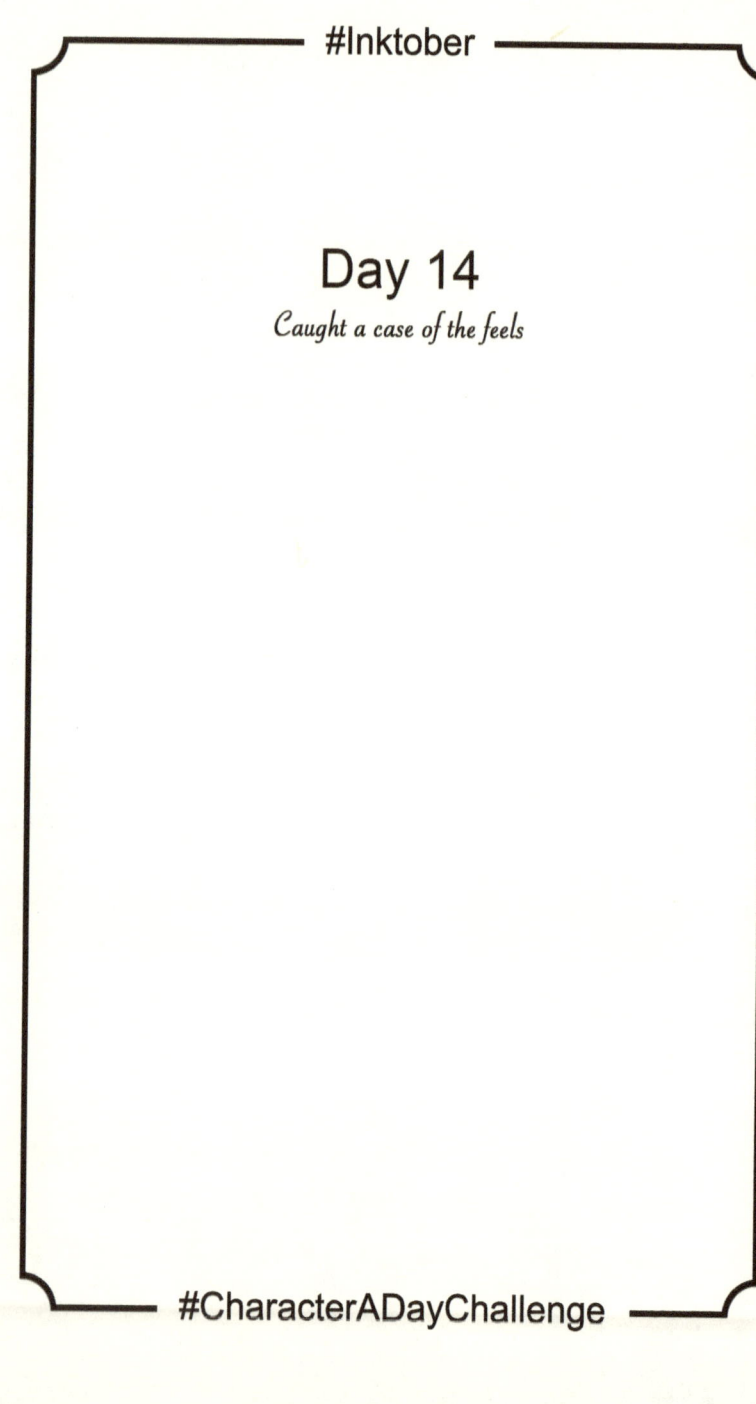

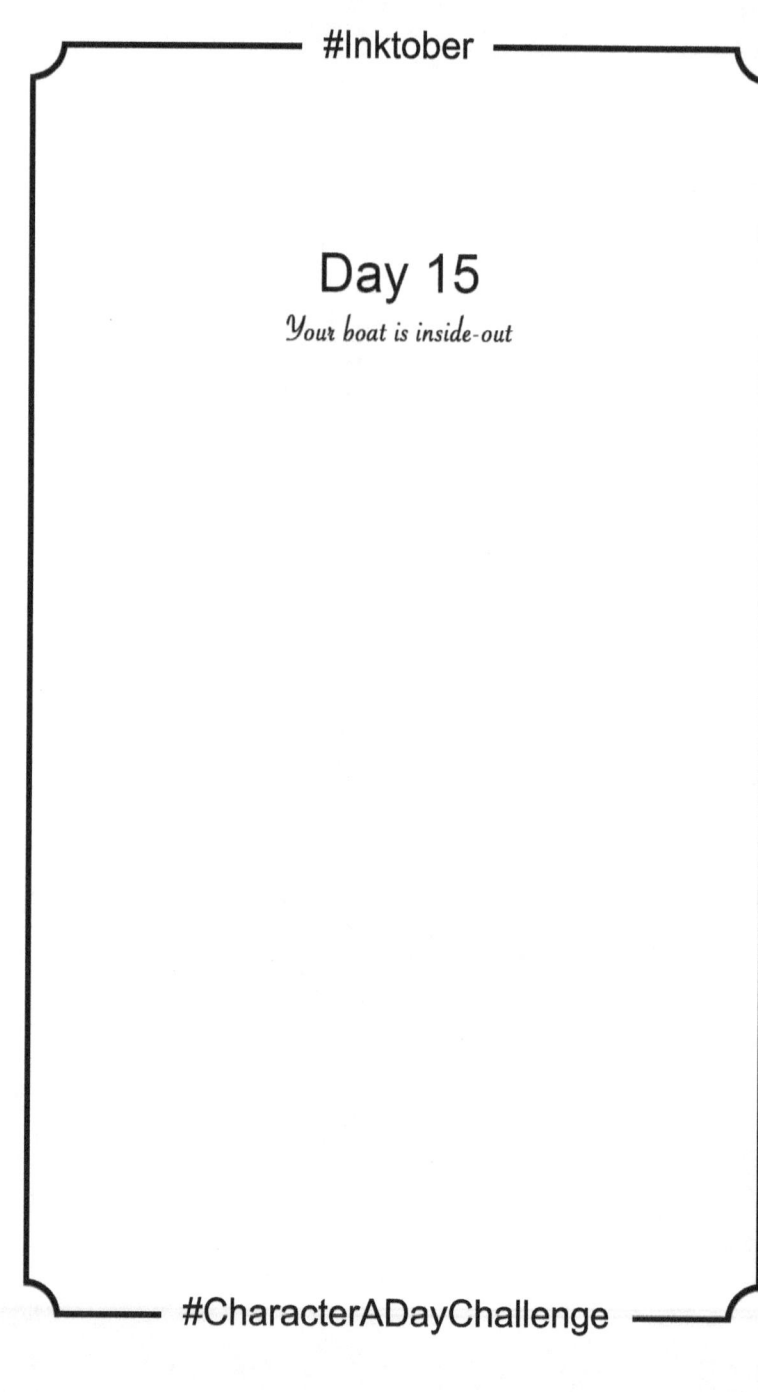

#Inktober

Day 16
The final's frontier

#CharacterADayChallenge

Day 17
What is the God box?

#Inktober

#CharacterADayChallenge

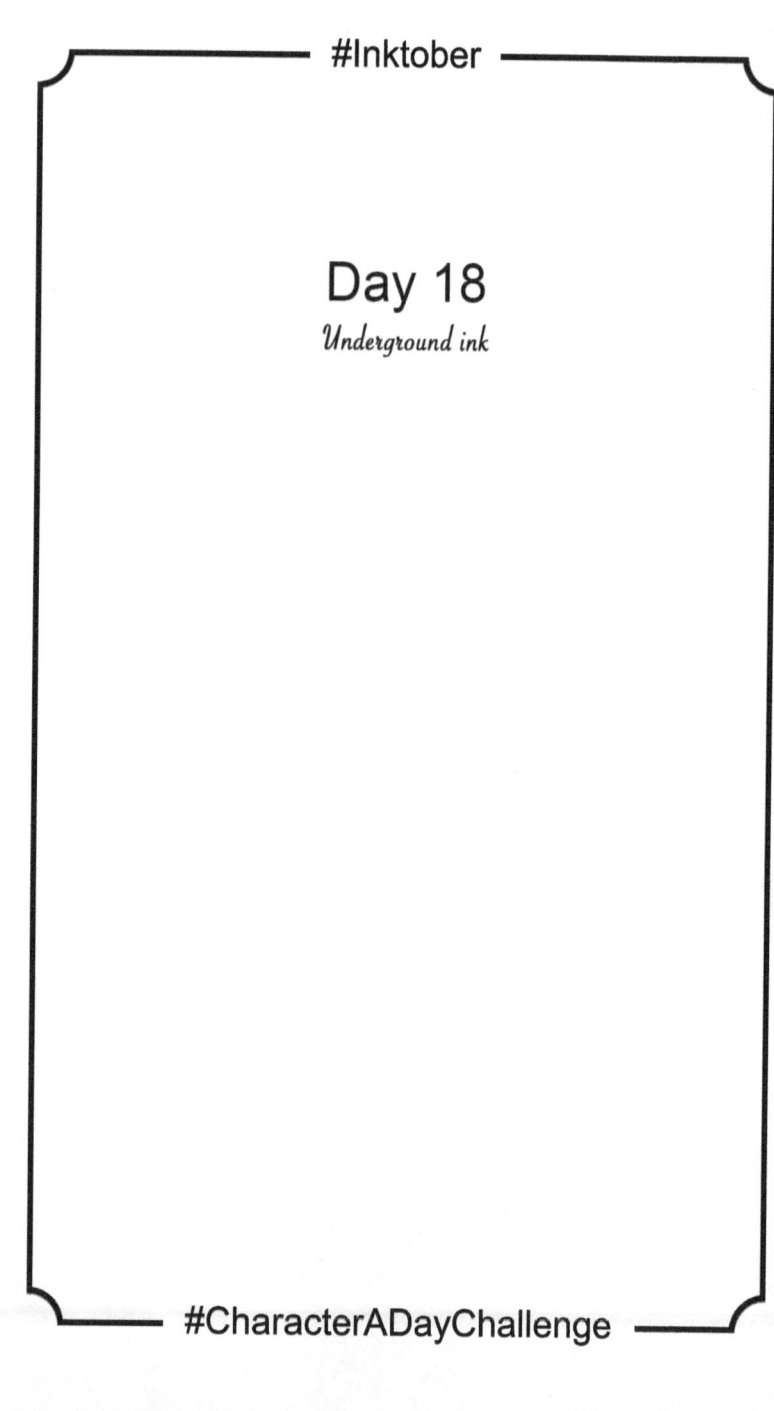

#Inktober

Day 19
I can only see the A.I.

#CharacterADayChallenge

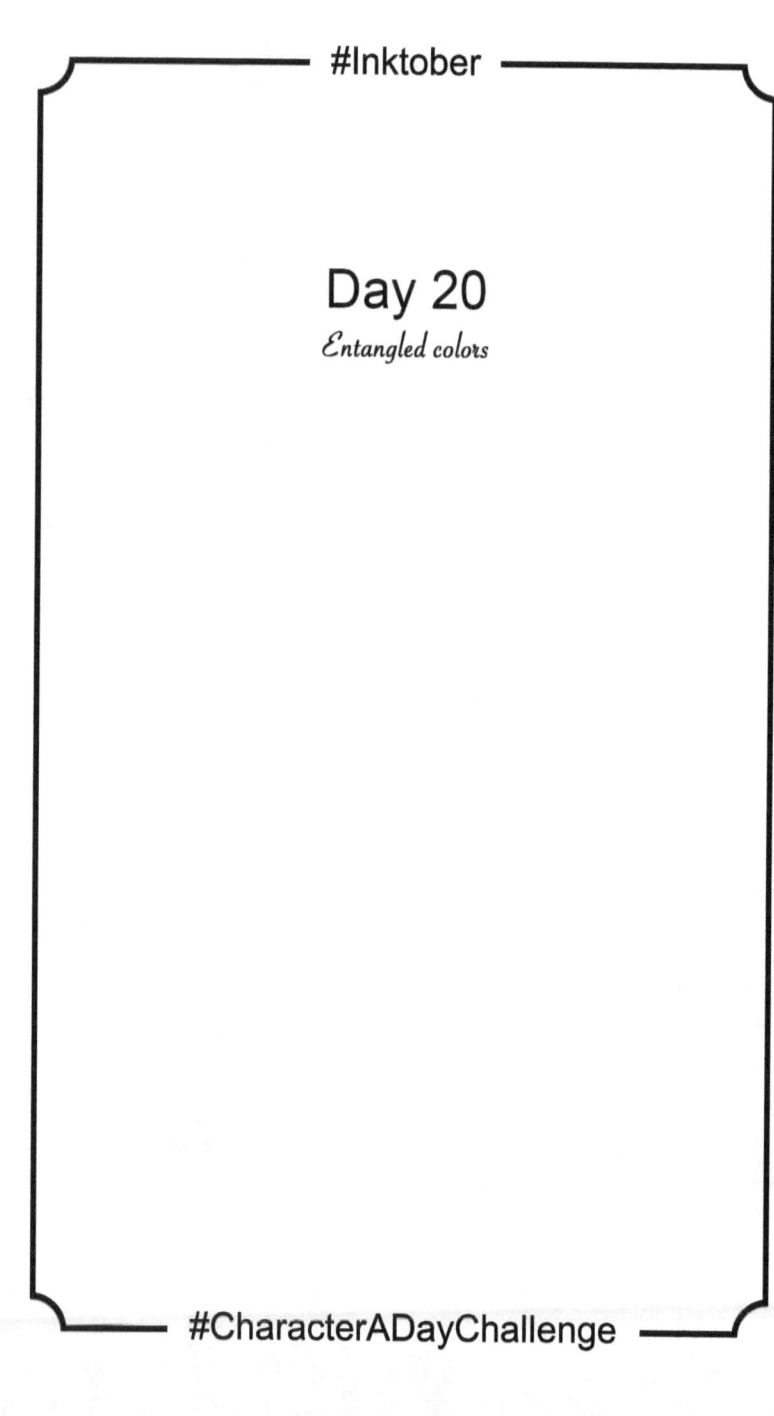

#Inktober

Day 21
Muse of limitations

#CharacterADayChallenge

#Inktober

Day 22
Today is tomorrow's future

#CharacterADayChallenge

#Inktober

Day 23
Fight the power

#CharacterADayChallenge

… #Inktober

Day 24
Zippers fall when they can't get up

#CharacterADayChallenge

#Inktober

Day 25
Be yourself, unless you're a twin

#CharacterADayChallenge

#Inktober

Day 26
Can you fall in a circle?

#CharacterADayChallenge

Day 27
8 fingers and tears

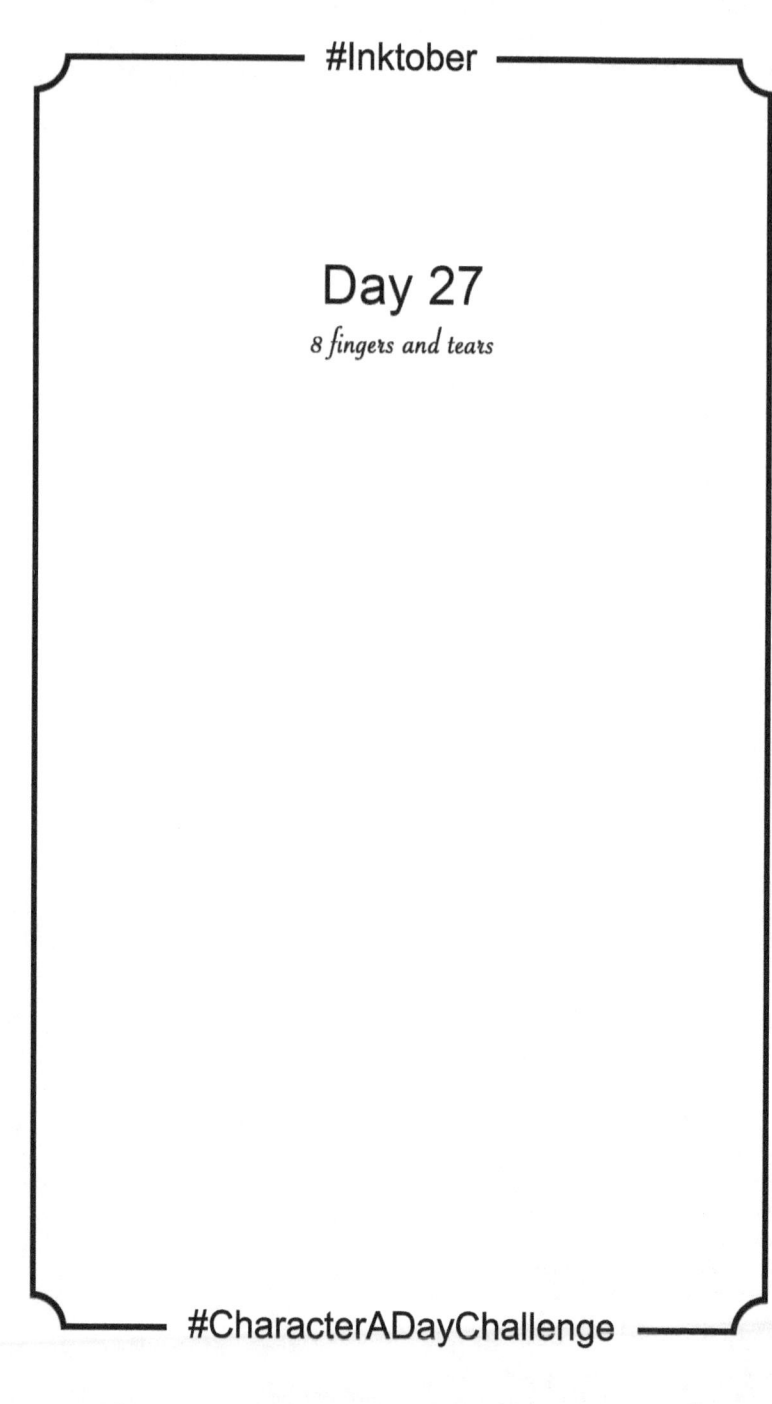

#Inktober

Day 28
History feels real somehow

#CharacterADayChallenge

#Inktober

Day 29
The lightning mountian is not a fountian

#CharacterADayChallenge

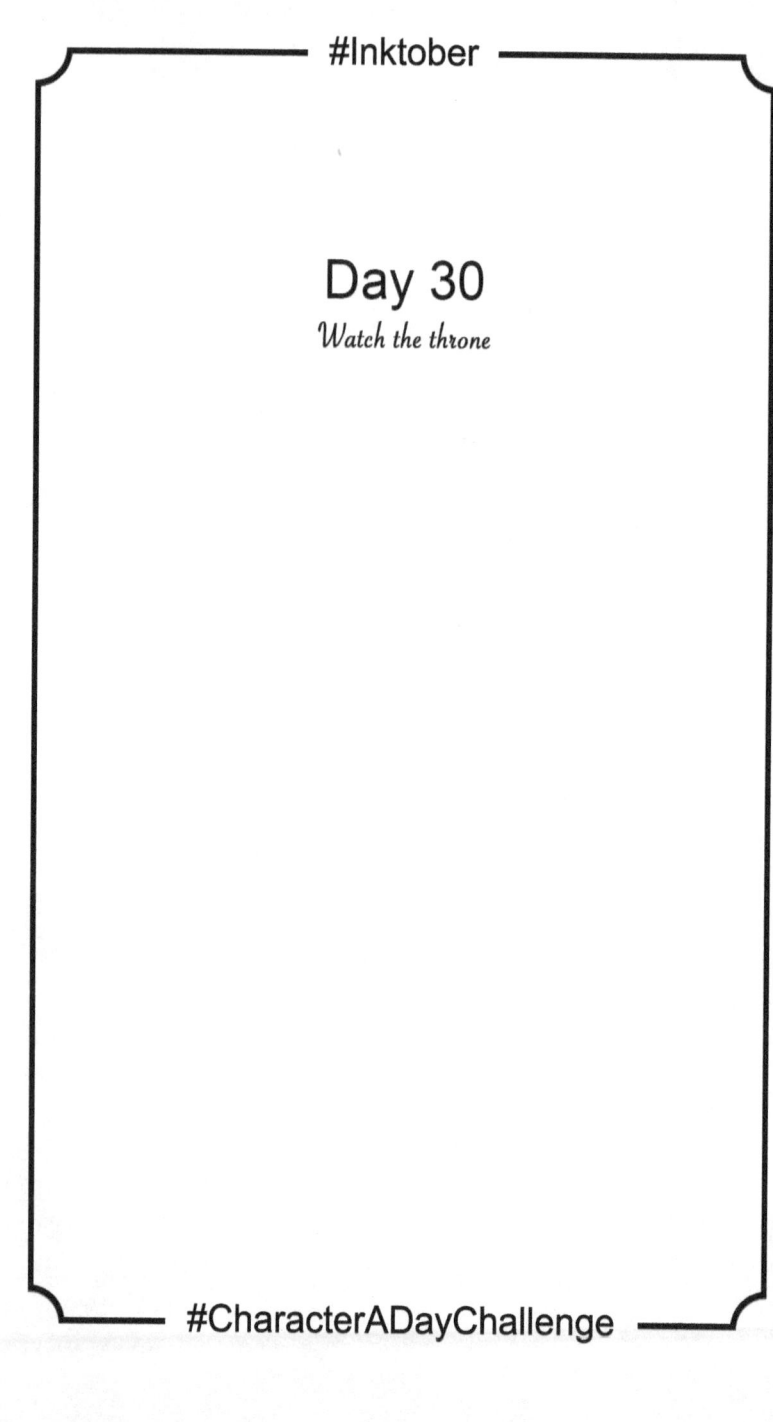

#Inktober

Day 31
Terror has a name

#CharacterADayChallenge

You made it!
Congrats on not letting this month beat you. We look forward to seeing your work online. Please follow us on Facebook @MyDailyHashtagChallenge and let us know what you thought of this book and others. Peace, love, and art forever!

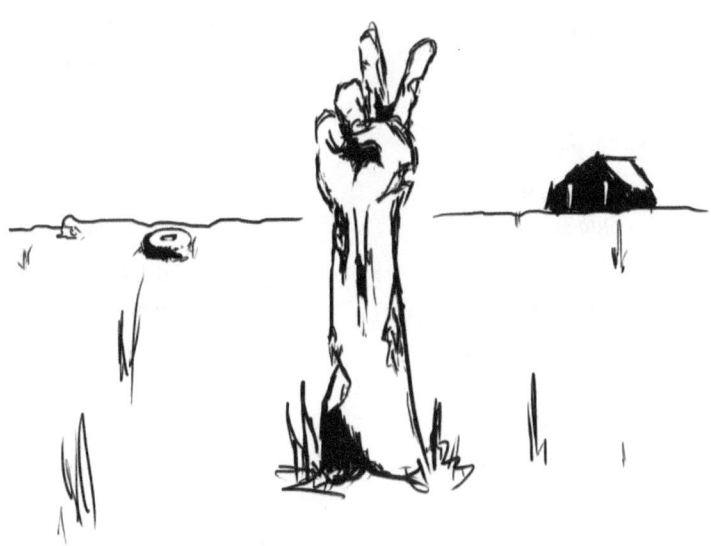

Day 1
What is that in the mirror?

Day 2
Fear me

Day 3
Find the warrior maid of glasses

Day 4
It's always darkest before the dawn

Day 5
Food for thought

Day 6
Sunday candy

Day 7
Make your own sound bagel

Day 8
The deeper you are

Day 9
Life is a garden

Day 10
Show me something natural

Day 11
These scars mean nothing

Day 12
I can see the finish line

Day 13
Pick your superpower

Day 14
Caught a case of the feels

Day 15
Your boat is inside-out

Day 16
The final's frontier

Day 17
What is the God box?

Day 18
Underground ink

Day 19
I can only see the A.I.

Day 20
Entangled colors

Day 21
Muse of limitations

Day 22
Today is tomorrow's future

Day 23
Fight the power

Day 24
Zippers fall when they can't get up

Day 25
Be yourself, unless you're a twin

Day 26
Can you fall in a circle?

Day 27
8 fingers and tears

Day 28
History feels real somehow

Day 29
The lightning mountain is not a fountain

Day 30
Watch the throne

Day 31
Terror has a name

Artists To Follow

A spotlight on inspirational inkers

Jake Parker
Inktober.com, IG- JakeParker, YT- Jake Parker

Chaim Hall
FB- Character A Day Challenge, IG- ChaimBurger

Travon Serrano
IG- TravonVon, YT- VonnyVon

Nikolas A. Draper-Ivey
IG- NikolasDraperIvey

Paper Frank
PaperFrank.com, FB- PaperFrank, IG- PaperFrank

Dan Flores
DaCreativeGenius.com, FB- Art Is King, IG- DaCreativeGenius

Marcus Williams
MarcusTheVisual.com, FB- Marcus The Visual, IG- MarcusTheVisual

Markus Prime
LeagueOfMLNN.com, IG- Markus.Effin.Prime

www.ingramcontent.com/pod-product-compliance
Lightning Source LLC
Chambersburg PA
CBHW031541210526
45464CB00003B/1089